Close-up Continents

Mapping Asia

Paul Rockett

★

with artwork by Mark Ruffle

W
FRANKLIN WATTS
LONDON•SYDNEY

Franklin Watts
First published in Great Britain in 2017 by
The Watts Publishing Group

Franklin Watts
An imprint of Hachette Children's Group
Part of The Watts Publishing Group
Carmelite House
50 Victoria Embankment
London EC4Y 0DZ

An Hachette UK Company.
www.hachette.co.uk

www.franklinwatts.co.uk

Executive editor: Adrian Cole
Series design and illustration: Mark Ruffle
www.rufflebrothers.com

Picture credits:
David Copeman/Alamy: 24cl; Bernardo Erti/
Dreamstime: 19br; Kojin/Shutterstock: 17bl;
Richard Powers/Corbis: 25tl; Rex/Shutterstock:
23tl; Lena Serditova/Shutterstock: 27c; Travel
mania/Shutterstock: 21tl; Vincentstthomas/
Dreamstime; 23b; Wikimedia Commons: 6-7;
World History Archive/Superstock: 5cl;
Zurijeta/Shutterstock: 27t.

Every attempt has been made to
clear copyright. Should there by any
inadvertent omission please apply to
the publisher for rectification.

Dewey number: 915
ISBN: 978 1 4451 4116 9

Printed in Malaysia

MIX
Paper from
responsible sources
FSC® C104740
FSC
www.fsc.org

Contents

Where is Asia?

Asia is the largest continent in the world. Its giant landmass borders Africa and Europe to the west and the Pacific Ocean to the east, where the continent is made up of thousands of islands.

ASIA

Landmass

Asia covers just under a third of all the land on Earth.

ASIA

Europe

Africa

Indian Ocean

Pacific Ocean

Locating Asia

We can describe the position of Asia in relation to the areas of land and water that surround it, as well as by using the points on a compass.

- Europe is west of Asia
- Northeast of Africa is Asia
- Asia is north of the Indian Ocean
- East of Asia is the Pacific Ocean

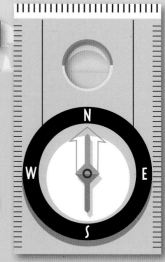

Continents are divided by natural features, such as mountain ranges or seas. Some geographers define a continent as being made up of one mass of land and therefore view Asia and Europe as a single continent, called Eurasia.

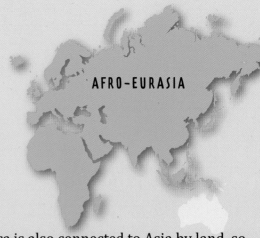

AFRO-EURASIA

EURASIA

Africa is also connected to Asia by land, so some people see the area as a supercontinent, called Afro-Eurasia or Eurafrasia.

Early map

The oldest known world map is from Asia and dates from around 600 BCE. It only shows a few territories, all within Asia. It was made in Babylon (now part of modern-day Iraq), which the map places in the centre of the world.

Mountains

Ocean

Habban

Urartu

Babylon

Ocean

Bit Yakin

Assyria

Der

Elam

Ocean

The map is a symbolic map of the world rather than a realistic interpretation. It mentions mythical creatures that connect the world to the heavens.

Mountains

Urartu

Assyria

Babylon

Babylonia

Der

Elam

This modern-day map shows the actual locations of the ancient places from the 600 BCE map.

5

Countries

Not only is Asia the largest continent in the world but it is also home to the world's largest countries and contains 60 per cent of the world's human population.

Transcontinental countries

There are five countries in Asia that also cross over into the continent of Europe. They are Russia, Azerbaijan, Georgia, Kazakhstan and Turkey. These are called 'transcontinental countries'.

Large and small

Russia is the largest country in the world, however only three-quarters of it is in Asia, with the remaining quarter in the continent of Europe.

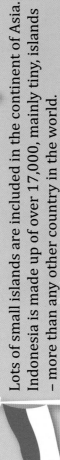

The largest country that lies wholly in Asia is China, covering around 20 per cent of Asia's landmass.

The smallest country in Asia is the Maldives. It is made up of a chain of islands in the Indian Ocean.

Lots of small islands are included in the continent of Asia. Indonesia is made up of over 17,000, mainly tiny, islands – more than any other country in the world.

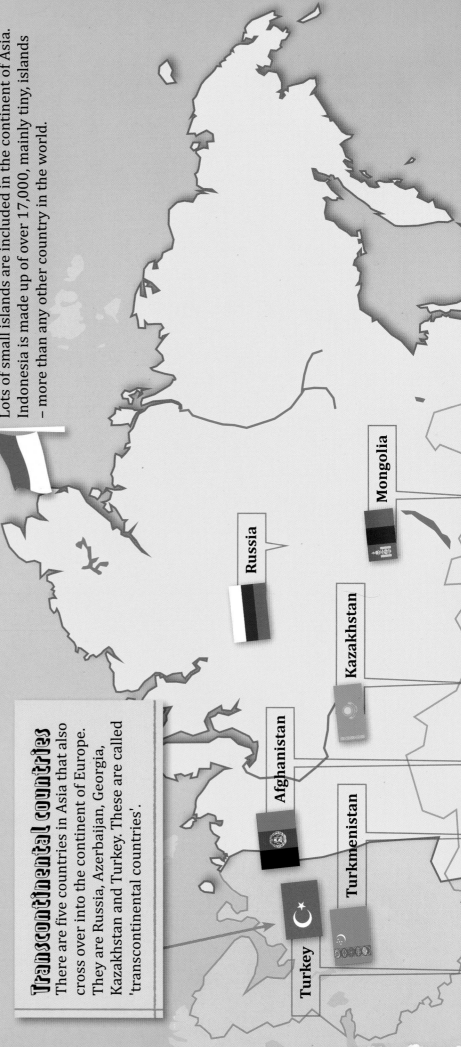

Russia

Mongolia

Kazakhstan

Afghanistan

Turkmenistan

Turkey

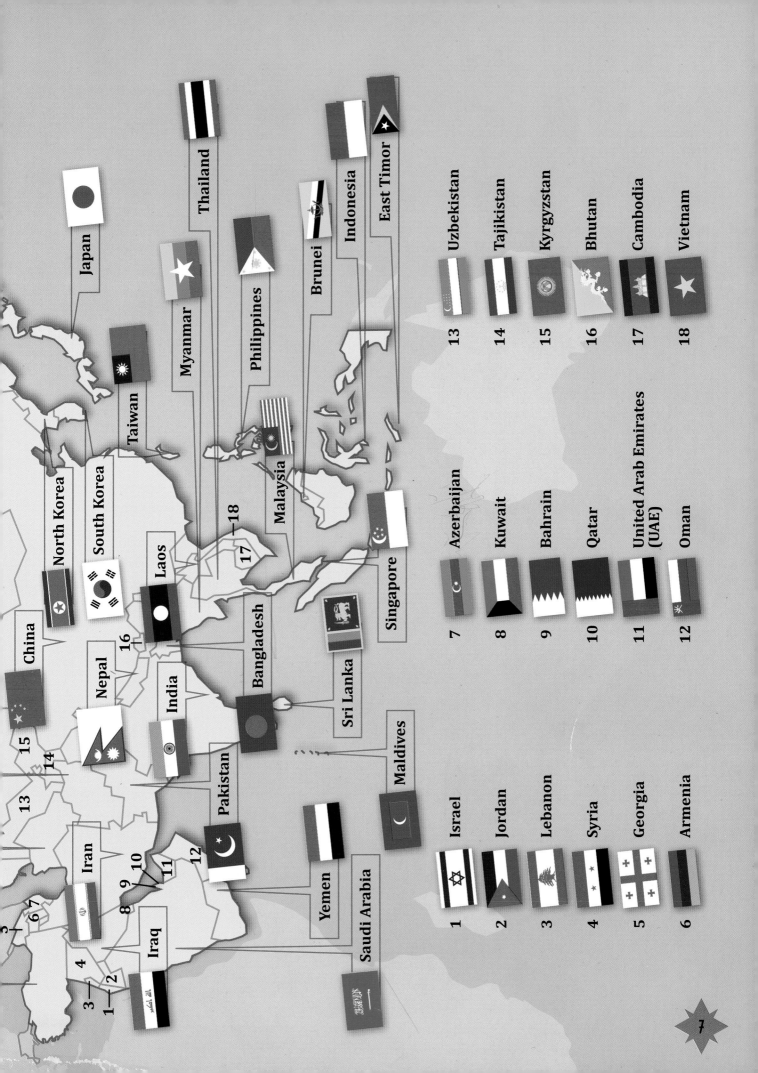

Japan

Thailand

Indonesia

East Timor

Brunei

Myanmar

Philippines

Taiwan

North Korea

South Korea

Laos

China

Nepal

India

Bangladesh

Sri Lanka

Malaysia

Singapore

Maldives

Pakistan

Iran

Iraq

Yemen

Saudi Arabia

—18

17

16

14

15

13

8 9 10 11

12

3

67

4

3 — 1 — 2

1 Israel

2 Jordan

3 Lebanon

4 Syria

5 Georgia

6 Armenia

7 Azerbaijan

8 Kuwait

9 Bahrain

10 Qatar

11 United Arab Emirates (UAE)

12 Oman

13 Uzbekistan

14 Tajikistan

15 Kyrgyzstan

16 Bhutan

17 Cambodia

18 Vietnam

Early civilisations

A civilisation is a well-organised society where people work together and have a shared culture. Many of the world's earliest civilisations can be found in Asia where they established the first cities and introduced inventions such as the wheel.

Sumerian Civilisation

Sumerian Civilisation 4500–1750 BCE

The Sumerians lived in the southern part of modern-day Iraq, between the Euphrates and Tigris rivers. This region was known as Sumer. Important inventions that have changed the course of history have come from here. These include the invention of the wheel, the first sailing boats and early forms of writing.

One of the first recorded works of literature comes from the Sumerians. It tells the story of Gilgamesh, a hero who fights a series of monsters in his search for the secret of eternal life.

The Sumerians built the first cities, building them around giant temples called 'ziggurats'.

What happened to them?

Attackers from Elam, a neighbouring area (now part of modern-day Iran), ransacked the cities and destroyed Sumer. The land was taken over by Elamites and Amorites (from modern-day Syria), followed by other civilisations. Many of the Sumerian cities were left in ruins.

Shang Dynasty

Indus Valley

Shang Dynasty
1600–1046 BCE

The Shang were a dynasty of kings who ruled an area of northern China over 12,000 years ago. Their people were skilled workers in bronze, bone, ivory, jade, stone, ceramics and tortoiseshell. They developed a calendar and also China's first writing system.

Indus Valley
3300–1700 BCE

The Indus Valley civilisation grew up along the banks of the River Indus, in what is now Pakistan and northwest India. It was one of the largest ancient civilisations with over 1,400 towns and cities. The Indus Valley people were advanced in urban-planning, designing cities in a grid pattern, building houses out of solid bricks and installing bathrooms with underground plumbing.

King Tang of Shang was the first king of the Shang Dynasty.

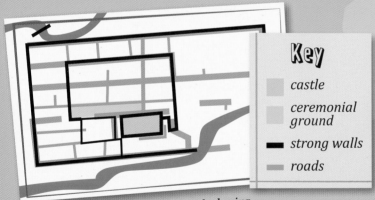

Key
- castle
- ceremonial ground
- strong walls
- roads

The Indus Valley city of Dholavira

The Shang were masters in the art of bronze casting, and produced elaborately decorated musical instruments and ceremonial vessels, as well as weapons, like this axe head.

What happened to them?

No one really knows what caused the end of the Indus Valley civilisation. Some think that:
– the land turned to desert, causing people to starve or move away;
– water levels rose along the River Indus, flooding the land;
– they faced an invasion by another civilisation and since the Indus people were peaceful, they would not have survived in battle.

What happened to them?

In the final years of the Shang Dynasty, there were frequent wars with rival kingdoms in China. They were finally defeated in battle by the Zhou Dynasty.

Regions

The countries within Asia can be grouped together into regions where they share political, religious and cultural histories, or a similar location.

Northern Asia

Northern Asia is made up of the Asian territory of Russia, east of the Ural Mountains. This area is sometimes referred to by its original name: Siberia.

Central Asia

Central Asia is made up of five countries that all end in '-stan' (meaning 'land of'). They are: Kazakhstan, Kyrgyzstan, Tajikistan, Turkmenistan and Uzbekistan. These countries were part of the Soviet Union until 1991.

Ural Mountains

Northern Asia

Caspian Sea

Central Asia

Aegean Sea

Black Sea

Himalayas

Southern Asia

Western Asia

Persian Gulf

Mediterranean Sea

Red Sea

Arabian Sea

Middle East

Western Asia

The region of Western Asia is surrounded by seven seas: the Aegean Sea, the Black Sea, the Caspian Sea, the Persian Gulf, the Arabian Sea, the Red Sea and the Mediterranean Sea. It includes a region known as 'the Middle East'.

The Middle East

The Middle East was originally named by foreign colonial powers to distinguish the region from nearby India. Here there are many societies with different traditions and religions of which Islam is the dominant religious and cultural influence.

The Fertile Crescent

Within the Middle East is a region known as 'the Fertile Crescent'. This curved area of land crosses through Iraq, Kuwait, Syria, Lebanon, Jordan, Israel, and into Egypt (in Africa). The land is perfect for growing crops, a feature that led to it being home to many of the world's first civilisations (see pages 8–9).

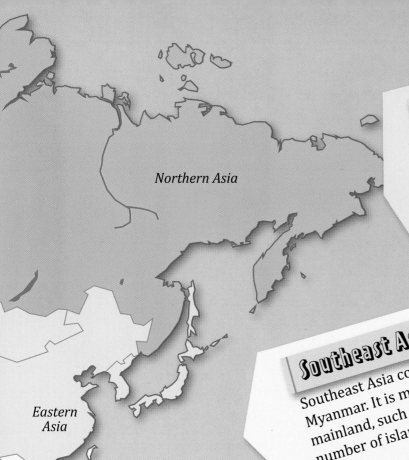

Northern Asia

Eastern Asia

Southeast Asia

Eastern Asia

Eastern Asia is dominated by the country of China and surrounding territories that have been influenced by the early Chinese dynasties. This includes Mongolia to the north, North and South Korea and the islands of Japan.

Southeast Asia

Southeast Asia covers an area south of China and east of Myanmar. It is made up of countries that connect it to the mainland, such as Thailand and Vietnam, as well as a large number of islands.

Southern Asia

Southern Asia covers land south of the Himalayas while stretching west to include Afghanistan and Iran. Within Southern Asia is a region known as the Indian Subcontinent.

Indian Subcontinent

The Indian Subcontinent

This region is characterised by its distinct landmass known as a peninsula – an area of land that sticks out from the mainland and is surrounded by water.

Countries are grouped within this region through geographic and historic connections. This includes countries that border India and those directly south of the Himalayas. It also includes countries that were once under the colonial control of British India, such as Bhutan and Myanmar.

Climates

Asia sits within both the Arctic Circle and the tropics. As a result the continent is home to some of the coldest and hottest places in the world, as well as some of the driest and wettest.

Asia's climate zones:

- polar
- subarctic
- highland
- humid continental
- Mediterranean
- dry
- tropical

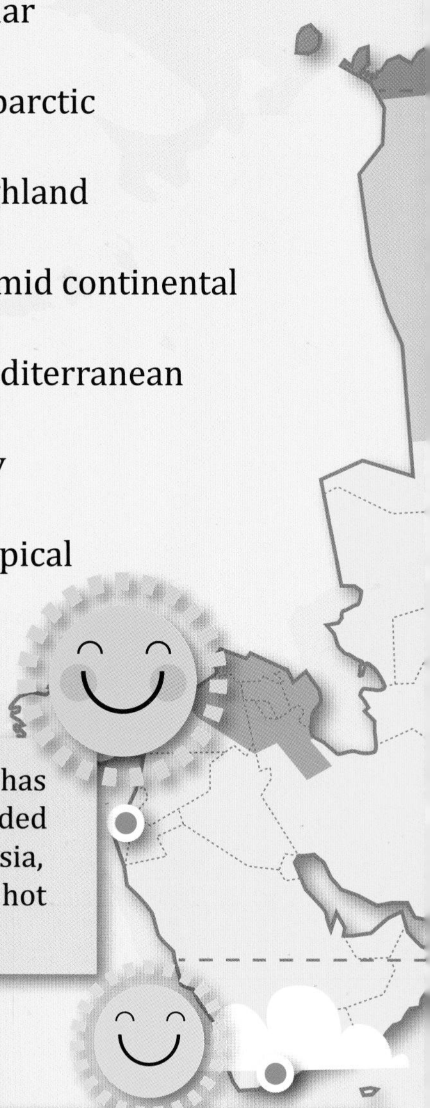

Contrasting climates

The polar climate in the north of Russia creates treeless plains, where the soil is permanently frozen. In contrast, the heat and humidity of the tropical climate in the south of Asia creates dense rainforests.

HIMALAYAS

Wettest place on Earth

Mawsynram, a town in India, is known to be the wettest place on Earth.

In this part of northeast India, rainclouds get trapped by the world's highest mountain range, the Himalayas, and are unable to escape further north.

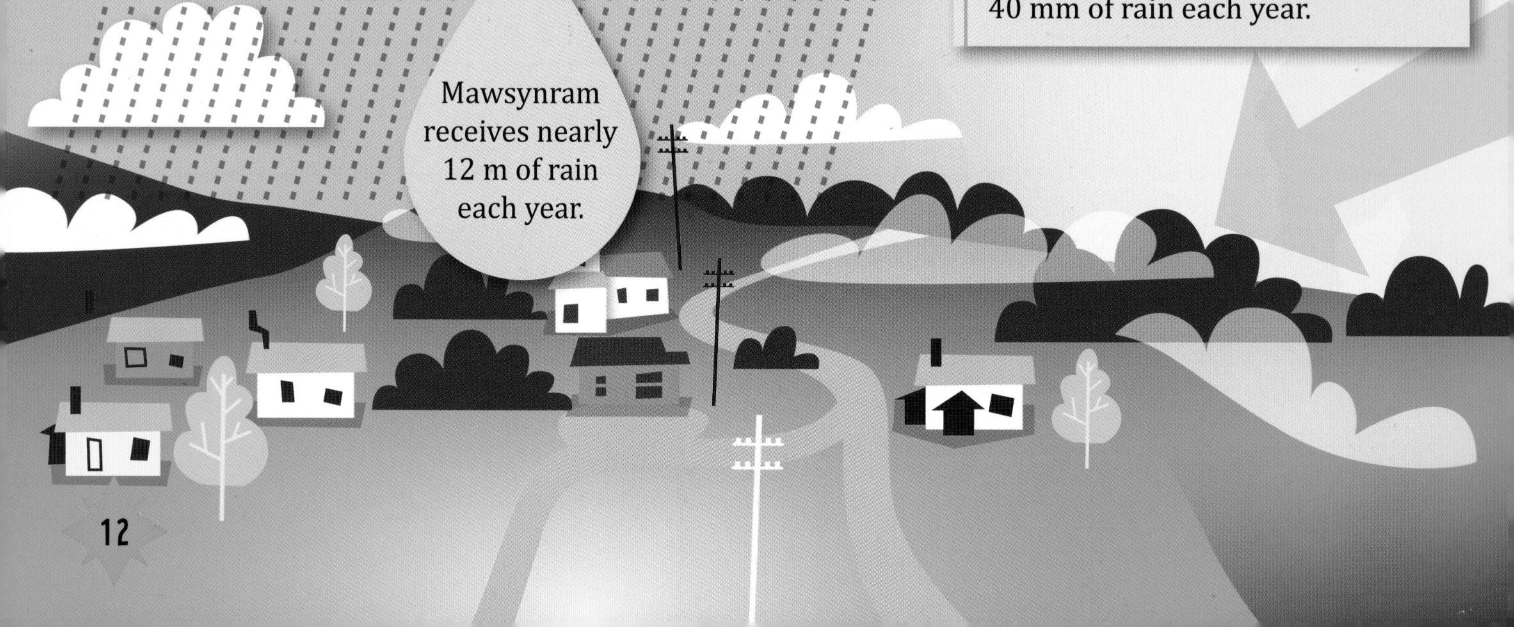

Tirat Tsvi, Israel, has the highest recorded temperature in Asia, with it getting as hot as 53.9°C.

Aden, in Yemen, is the driest place in Asia. It receives on average only 40 mm of rain each year.

Mawsynram receives nearly 12 m of rain each year.

Arctic Circle

Verkhoyansk, Russia, has the record for being the coldest place in Asia, with temperatures dropping to -67.8°C.

Monsoon seasons

Monsoon season occurs when strong winds change direction. Monsoon winds blow in from cold to warm places, carrying moisture or cool, drying air. The climate in the Indian Subcontinent is ruled by wet and dry monsoon seasons.

Highland climate

This mountainous area has a highland climate, where the weather is cool to cold.

Himalayas

Tropic of Cancer

Mawsynram

Equator

Summer monsoon

From June to September, winds blow moist air from the Indian Ocean to bring heavy rainfall to parts of India, Sri Lanka and Bangladesh.

Indian Ocean

Winter monsoon

From October, the winds change direction, bringing dry, sunny weather to most of the Indian Subcontinent, although the far southeast of the peninsular does experience a second shorter wet monsoon from October to December.

Wildlife

Many strange and beautiful animals and plants can only be found living wild in Asia. Hiding in mountain forests or roaming freely on islands and open plains, many of these creatures have become symbols of their region.

Arctic hare

Brown bear

Camels

There are two species of camel: the Bactrian camel (two humps) and the dromedary camel (one hump), both of which can be found in Asia. Camels store fat in their humps, which can be converted into energy and water when no food supplies are available. This makes them the perfect animal for long journeys across deserts.

While most camels in Asia are used for transporting goods, there are some Bactrian camels living wild in the Gobi Desert, across Mongolia and China.

Gobi Desert

China

Bengal tiger

Sumatran rhinoceros

Borneo

Sumatra

Dromedary camel

Komodo dragon

The Komodo dragon is the world's largest lizard and only lives wild on five Indonesian islands. They can grow up to 3 m in length and weigh more than 136 kg. They feast on animals ranging in size from small mice to large water buffalos.

Flores

Rinca

Komodo

Gili Motang

Gili Dasami

Taiga forest

The taiga forest in the north of Russia is one of the largest forested areas in the world. It makes up around one-half of the world's evergreen forests. It is also one of the coldest areas of Asia, and animals that live here, such as Arctic hares, grow thick fur coats to help them survive the harsh winter months.

Bamboo

Bamboo is one of the fastest growing plants in the world – some bamboo can grow as much as one metre in 24 hours! Bamboo plants can also grow very tall, some reaching 35 m in height.

Bamboo is an important plant for the economy in East and Southeast Asia. It's used as a building material, for food, for making furniture and there are even bamboo bikes and skateboards.

Rafflesia arnoldii

The rafflesia arnoldii is the largest known flower in the world. It can grow up to 1 m across. The flower is also one of the nastiest smelling, giving off an aroma of rotting meat.

Giant panda

The giant panda is an endangered species. There are only around 1,600 left in the wild.

Giant pandas live mainly in bamboo forests high in the mountains of western China. Their diet is approximately 99 per cent bamboo. They can eat up to 14 kg of bamboo shoots a day – and poo up to 40 times a day!

Orangutan

Orangutans are found in the tropical rainforests of Sumatra and Borneo. The name orangutan means 'man of the forest' in the Malay language. They are dependent on the forest for shelter and food, spending around 90 per cent of their time up in the trees.

Natural landmarks

The vast landscape of Asia contains the world's highest mountains, large deserts and curious sites of stone forests, white terraces and salty lakes.

The Dead Sea

The Dead Sea is between Israel and Jordan. Although called a sea, it's really a lake, with water flowing into it from the River Jordan.

The Dead Sea is also known as the Salt Sea, as there is so much salt in the water that people can float in it.

Sea level

The Dead Sea is the lowest spot on the Earth's land surface at 417 m below sea level.

The Himalayas

The Himalayas is a mountain range that crosses through Pakistan, India, China, Nepal and Bhutan. It's the highest mountain range on Earth, containing 9 out of 10 of the world's highest peaks, including the world's highest mountain, Mount Everest.

Manaslu 8,156 m

Cho Oyu 8,201 m

Everest 8,848 m

Lhotse 8,516 m

Makalu 8,462 m

A section of the Himalayas.

K2 is the second highest mountain in the world. It is 8,611 m high and is between China and Pakistan in the Karakoram mountain range.

Lake Baikal

Caspian Sea

16

Mount Fuji

Mount Fuji is a symbol of Japan. It's the country's tallest mountain, measuring 3,776 m in height. It's also an active volcano, although it last erupted in 1707.

Gobi Desert

The Gobi Desert is a cold, rocky desert and only around 5 per cent of it is covered in sand. It is an important area for fossil finds – dinosaur eggs were first discovered here.

The Yangtze is 6,300 km long. It's the longest river in Asia and the third longest river in the world.

Gobi Desert

Himalayas

Karakum Desert

Thar Desert

Arabian Desert

Pamukkale

Pamukkale, meaning 'cotton castle' in Turkish, is an area that contains terraces with a bright white foamy appearance. This is created by deposits of calcium carbonate that bubble up from hot springs.

Shilin Stone Forest

In the Yunnan Province of China is an area of land covered with hundreds of tall rocks, some reaching up to 30 m in height. The rocks were carved out by over 270 million years of earthquakes, wind and water erosion, and look like a dense forest made of stone.

Manmade landmarks

From the awe-inspiring ancient structures of the past to the towering heights of the modern-day, Asia is home to some of the world's most breath-taking and record-breaking architecture.

City of Petra

The city of Petra in Jordan is made up of temples, tombs, theatres and houses that are half-built and half-carved into rock. Petra has existed for over 2,000 years; it is one of the world's largest archaeological sites and is filled with the remains of past Arabic and Mediterranean civilisations.

It's thought that Petra was established as a meeting point for different trade routes, with camels transporting spices and other goods between the Mediterranean, Africa, Middle East and India.

Burj Khalifa

The Burj Khalifa in Dubai is the tallest man-made structure in the world. It stands at 829.8 m tall, and from the top you can see the whole of Dubai and even as far as the neighbouring country of Iran.

Taj Mahal

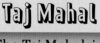

The Taj Mahal, in the northern city of Agra, is the most popular tourist attraction in India. It was built between 1631 and 1648 for the grief-stricken emperor Shah Jahan, as a tomb for his third and favourite wife, Mumtaz Mahal.

The four sides of the building appear identical with a repeated pattern of large arches and domes.

The building is made from white marble that appears to change colour at different times of the day.

Great Wall of China

The Great Wall of China is the world's longest wall, stretching across China for 21,196 km. It was built by many different emperors over a long time period to keep out invaders.

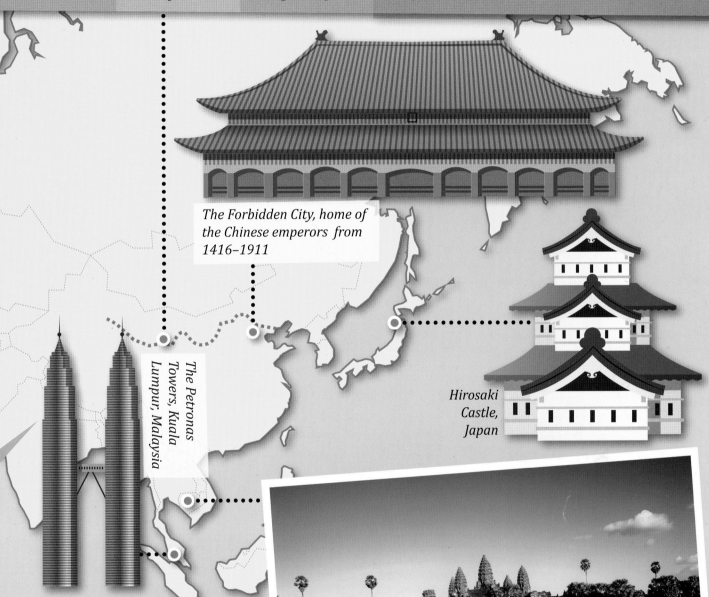

The Forbidden City, home of the Chinese emperors from 1416–1911

The Petronas Towers, Kuala Lumpur, Malaysia

Hirosaki Castle, Japan

Angkor

Angkor is a large site in Cambodia that contains the remains of capital cities that existed from the 9th to the 15th century. The area is filled with ancient temples, canals and traces of over 112 historic settlements.

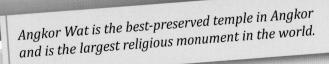

Angkor Wat is the best-preserved temple in Angkor and is the largest religious monument in the world.

19

Industry

Over half of the population of Asia earn their living through farming. Manufacturing and fuel industries are also big employers, with large companies and resources supplying the continent – and the rest of the world – with energy, fashion items and electronics.

Main industries in Asia

Crops:

Rice

Sugar

Tea

Fruit

Wheat

Cotton

Industry:

Manufacturing/Industrial Areas

Forestry

Hi-tech

Fishing

Textiles

Tourism

Livestock:

Cattle

Sheep

Pigs

Energy:

Oil

Natural gas

Hydroelectricity

Coal

Nuclear

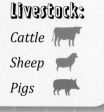

Oil and gas

At least 60 per cent of the world's known oil and gas deposits are found in Asia, most notably the oil fields of the Persian Gulf. The discovery of oil here in the 1930s brought great wealth to countries with a Persian Gulf coastline: Iran, Saudi Arabia, UAE, Kuwait, Qatar and Bahrain. Combined, these countries supply one-fifth of the world with oil.

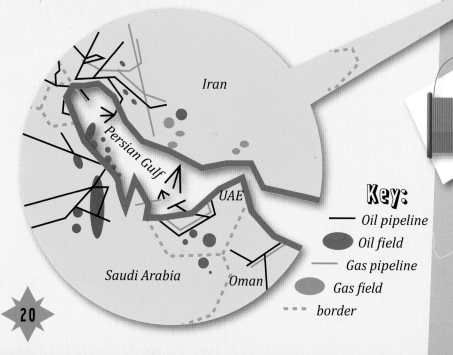

Iran

Persian Gulf

UAE

Saudi Arabia

Oman

Key:

— Oil pipeline

⬭ Oil field

— Gas pipeline

⬬ Gas field

--- border

Textiles

The textile industry is key to the economies and employment of workers in India and Bangladesh. They are two of the world's biggest textile exporters.

78 per cent of Bangladesh's export earnings come from textiles

India has more land set aside for growing cotton than any other country in the world

Rice farming

The most important crop in Asia is rice. More than 90 per cent of the world's rice is produced and consumed here. The Chinese people grow and eat the most rice in the world, followed by the people of India, Indonesia, Bangladesh, Vietnam, Philippines and Myanmar.

Most rice is grown in paddy fields; these are man-made ponds that are built into the landscape in rows, often into steep hillsides.

Electronics

Towards the end of the twentieth century, Japan was the number one country for manufacturing electronic goods. It introduced the handheld camcorder, CD player and Nintendo Game Boy. However, South Korea has begun to steal Japan's position as the top exporter of electronic goods. South Korea is home to Samsung Electronics, the world's largest technology company and largest manufacturer of mobile phones.

Hydroelectricity

Hydroelectricity is a renewable energy and accounts for around 16 per cent of the world's electricity.

China is the world's largest producer and has the world's largest hydroelectric power station, the Three Gorges Dam. Built on the Yangtze River, the dam stretches around 1.3 km across and is 181 m high.

Hydroelectricity produces electricity through the gravitational force of falling or flowing water

Dams channel and direct the force of water

The water turns turbines, which then generate electricity

Three Gorges Dam

Settlements

Asia is the most populated continent in the world. It's estimated that three out of every five people on Earth live in Asia. While there are many large areas of land and islands where hardly anyone lives, most of the population is crammed into urban areas, with Asia being home to the world's most overcrowded cities.

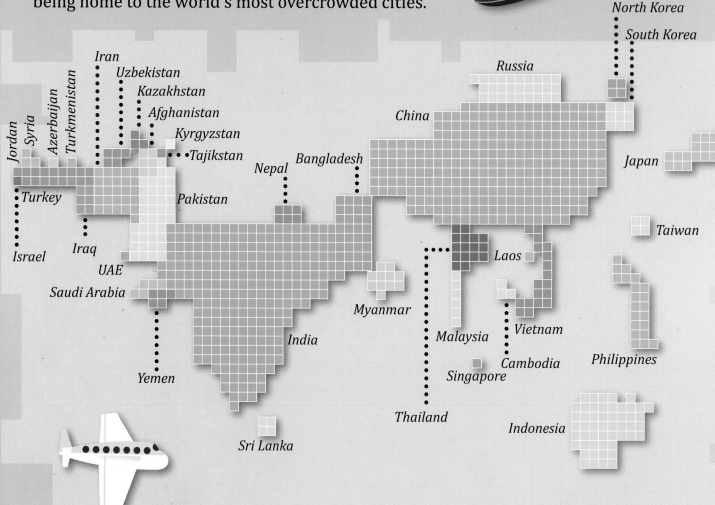

Population map

This is a population map of Asia, where the size of each country is shown in proportion to its population. Each square represents 5 million people; countries with a population under 5 million are not shown. This makes China appear as the largest country even though it is smaller in size than Russia.

Palm Island, United Arab Emirates

Palm Island is attached to the mainland of Dubai, in the United Arab Emirates. It's an artificial island constructed from sand dredged up from the bottom of the Persian Gulf, shaped like a palm tree with a surrounding crescent. The island was completed in 2006, taking five years to build, and measures 5 km by 5 km.

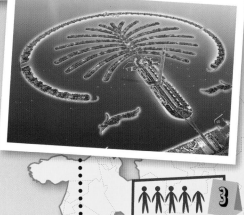

Mongolia

A third of Mongolians live in the capital city Ulan Bator, while the rest inhabit smaller urban areas or farmland. Historically, Mongolians were a nomadic people who roamed freely across the land. A small minority still live this lifestyle, and move across the vast western area of grassland and shrubland, known as steppe. They herd cattle and live in tents called gers, moving their homes around in trucks where in the past they would have used ox and carts.

Ger

Megacities

A megacity is an urban area with a population of more than 10 million. Out of the top ten largest megacities in the world, nine are Asian.
Largest cities in Asia:

1 Tokyo, Japan 37.8 million people

2 Jakarta, Indonesia 30.5 million people

3 Delhi, India 24.9 million people

4 Manila, Philippines 24.1 million people

5 Seoul, South Korea 23.48 million people

Key: 🧍 = five million people

Tokyo skyline

Sport

In countries across Asia, people display great passion for a wide variety of sports, some of which are unique to the area. Many of their sports have developed as a result of a country's history, religion or wildlife.

Rhythmic gymnastics

The most popular sport for girls in Russia is rhythmic gymnastics. This sport involves an individual or small team performing a routine that combines elements of ballet, gymnastics and dance. The routines usually involve a piece of apparatus such as a ball, hoop or ribbon.

Martial arts

Eastern Asia is home to many of the world's most-practised martial arts. Although more commonly seen as a set of skills for self-defence, competitions and action movie fight scenes, many of the martial arts developed out of ancient philosophies. They have a focus on spiritual and mental development that is still valued today.

Kendo

Japan is home to martial arts that are popular all over the world, such as judo and karate. It's also the country where kendo comes from. Kendo means 'way of the sword' and has developed over 1,000 years. Opponents fight each other using a bamboo sword (called a shinai), while dressed in protective armour.

Kendo position:
a 'rei' (bow) performed
before combat begins

Camel racing

Camel racing has existed in Arab countries since the 7th century CE, but became a professional sport only within the last 100 years. United Arab Emirates is the centre of camel racing in Asia, housing top training grounds with treadmills and swimming pools to exercise their highly-prized racing camels.

Taekwondo

Taekwondo is the national sport of South Korea. The name Taekwondo breaks down to mean (*Tae*) foot, (*Kwon*) hand, (*Do*) art. The hands and feet are mainly used to overcome an opponent.

Taekwondo move: flying side kick

Shaolin Kung Fu

Shaolin Kung Fu has existed for over 1,500 years and was originally practised by Buddhist monks in the Henan province of China. It began as a series of exercises built around meditation and developed into skills used for self-defence.

Shaolin Kung Fu position: the horse stance

Jakarta

113

Cricket

Cricket is more popular in India and Pakistan than anywhere else in the world. It was introduced to the area by the British in the 1700s, and has gone on to obsess both countries, producing some of the world's greatest cricket players.

Asian Games

The Asian Games takes place once every four years, with 45 nations from the continent competing in a number of different sports, including swimming, table tennis and basketball. It's the second-largest multi-sporting event in the world, second to the Olympic Games. The first Asian Games took place in New Delhi, India in 1951; the next event will be held in 2018, in Jakarta, Indonesia.

Culture

The main religions from around the world all started in Asia, and many of its cities have strong cultural connections to different faiths. The continent's religious and traditional festivals are celebrated all around the world as is its reputation and history for performing arts.

Judaism

Judaism, the religion of the Jews, began over 3,500 years ago, in a place called Canaan. This was once a large country that covered parts of present-day Lebanon, Syria, Jordan and Israel.

Lebanon
Syria
CANAAN
Israel
Iraq
Jordan
Saudi Arabia
Egypt

Russian ballet

Ballet is popular throughout all of Russia and the Russian State Ballet is based in its Asian territory, in Krasnoyarsk.

Krasnoyarsk

Islam

It's traditionally thought that Islam began in 610 CE, when the archangel Jibril visited Muhammad (peace be upon him) on the Jabal al-Nour mountain, near Makkah.

Varanasi

Sikhism

Sikhism was founded in the Punjab province of northern India in the 15th century CE, by the teachings of Guru Nanak.

Christianity

Christianity began over 2,000 years ago with the birth of Jesus Christ in Bethlehem, in the present-day Palestinian area of Israel.

Buddhism

Buddhism originated in northeast India in the 5th century BCE, beginning with the birth of Buddha.

Makkah

The Grand Mosque in Makkah

Makkah, in Saudi Arabia, is the birthplace of the Prophet Muhammad (pbuh). Wherever they are in the world, Muslims always pray facing Makkah. All Muslims are required to make a pilgrimage there at least once in their lifetime.

Hinduism

Varanasi is one of the most sacred sites for Hinduism, the dominant religion of India. Varanasi is often called the 'holy city of India'. It's home to over 20,000 temples, shrines and other places of worship. It has importance for Buddhism too, as it's believed that its founder, Buddha, began preaching near to the city.

Varanasi is one of the oldest cities on Earth that has been continually inhabited. It dates back to around 11–12th century BCE.

Chinese New Year

Chinese New Year is a major festival and holiday in China, and is also celebrated around the world in cities and countries where there are large Chinese populations. The celebrations begin at the turn of the Chinese calendar and last for 15 days.

Dragon dances are popular at New Year, with dancers holding aloft a dragon and moving it in time with music. The dragon is a Chinese symbol of good luck.

Shadow puppets

Shadow puppetry is popular in many Southeast Asian countries. The puppets have intricate designs with moveable body parts. They are held behind a white cloth, with a light shining behind them casting a shadow onto the cloth. The puppets are used to act out religious stories and folk tales.

Food and drink

Asian food and drink is popular all over the world, with Chinese takeaways, curry houses and sushi bars being common fixtures in most towns and cities. Often the ingredients of traditional recipes have been altered to suit more western tastes, but the authentic and original dishes can still be found in Asia where they are highly cherished.

Asian takeaway

SWEET AND SOUR PORK

One of the most popular Chinese dishes eaten around the world is sweet and sour pork. The sauce originates from the Canton province of Southern China. The ingredients include sugar that makes it sweet and rice vinegar that provides the sour taste.

VINDALOO CURRY

The curries that are eaten in Asia, from countries like India and Thailand, are often very different to those eaten in Asian restaurants outside of the continent. A chicken, prawn or lamb vindaloo is often the spiciest dish on a restaurant menu, but in Goa in India, where it originated, it is less spicy and is mainly served with pork.

SUSHI

Sushi is the name for a Japanese dish made up of small amounts of cold rice, flavoured with vinegar, often wrapped in seaweed, and topped with seafood, fish or vegetables or wrapped around fish and vegetables.

SUMMER ROLLS

A popular appetiser from Vietnam is the summer roll, also known as a salad roll. The rolls are full of prawns, bits of pork, vegetables and rice noodles, all wrapped together in rice paper 'rolls'. It is often served with dipping sauces tasting of chilli, peanut or sweet soy sauce.

Tea

After water, tea is the most widely drunk beverage in the world. The majority of the tea drunk today comes from countries in Asia, such as India, Sri Lanka and Indonesia. The largest producer of tea is China, where the history of tea drinking begins...

c. 2700 BCE

Legend has it that Chinese Emperor Shen Nong accidentally invented tea. While sat under a camellia sinensis tree, some leaves are believed to have fallen into his cup of hot water.

Tea is made from the leaves of the camellia sinensis tree.

900s

Tea drinking spreads to Japan, where the Tea Ceremony is created. The ceremony involves rituals around preparing the tea and the space in which it is drunk. These may vary depending on local customs, but the aim is to achieve a peaceful and serene experience.

c. 300 BCE

Tea becomes a daily drink in China.

1800s

British colonisers establish tea plantations in India. Today, India is the second biggest producer of tea, behind China.

1600s

Tea reaches Europe.

1980s

Bubble tea was invented in Taiwan in the 1980s but has only recently become popular around the rest of the world. This drink mixes tea with fruit juice or milk and contains either jellies or balls of tapioca. The drink is mostly served cold and is shaken up to create frothy bubbles.

COUNTRY	SIZE SQ KM	POPULATION	CAPITAL CITY	MAIN LANGUAGES
China	9,596,960	1,367,485,388	Beijing	Mandarin Chinese
India	3,287,263	1,251,695,584	New Delhi	Hindi, Bengali, English
Indonesia	1,904,569	255,993,674	Jakarta	Indonesian
Pakistan	796,095	199,085,847	Islamabad	Urdu, Punjabi, English
Bangladesh	148,460	168,957,745	Dhaka	Bengali
Russia	17,098,242 [including European territory]	142,423,773 [whole country]	Moscow	Russian
Japan	377,915	126,919,659	Tokyo	Japanese
Philippines	300,000	100,998,376	Manila	Filipino, English
Vietnam	331,210	94,348,835	Hanoi	Vietnamese
Iran	1,648,195	81,824,270	Tehran	Persian
Turkey	783,562 [including European territory]	79,414,269 [whole country]	Ankara	Turkish
Thailand	513,120	67,976,405	Bangkok	Thai
Myanmar	676,578	56,320,206	Naypyitaw	Burmese
South Korea	99,720	49,115,196	Seoul	Korean
Iraq	438,317	37,056,169	Baghdad	Arabic, Kurdish
Afghanistan	652,230	32,564,342	Kabul	Dari, Pashto
Nepal	147,181	31,551,305	Kathmandu	Nepali
Malaysia	329,847	30,513,848	Kuala Lumpur	Malay
Uzbekistan	447,400	29,199,942	Tashkent	Uzbek
Saudi Arabia	2,149,690	27,752,316	Riyadh	Arabic
Yemen	527,968	26,737,317	Sana'a	Arabic
North Korea	120,538	24,983,205	Pyongyang	Korean
Taiwan	35,980	23,415,126	Taipei	Mandarin Chinese
Sri Lanka	65,610	22,053,488	Sri Jayewardenapura Kotte, Colombo	Sinhala, Tamil
Kazakhstan	2,724,900 [including European territory]	18,157,122 [whole country]	Astana	Kazakh, Russian
Syria	185,180	17,064,854	Damascus	Arabic
Cambodia	181,035	15,708,756	Phnom Penh	Khmer
Azerbaijan	86,600 [including European territory]	9,780,780 [whole country]	Baku	Azerbaijani
Tajikistan	144,100	8,191,958	Dushanbe	Tajik
Jordan	89,342	8,117,564	Amman	Arabic
Israel	20,770	8,049,314	Jerusalem	Hebrew, Arabic
Laos	236,800	6,911,544	Vientiane	Lao
Lebanon	10,400	6,184,701	Beirut	Arabic
United Arab Emirates	83,600	5,779,760	Abu Dhabi	Arabic
Singapore	697	5,674,472	Singapore	Mandarin, English, Malay
Kyrgyzstan	199,951	5,664,939	Bishkek	Kyrgyz, Russian
Turkmenistan	488,100	5,231,422	Ashgabat	Turkmen
Georgia	69,700 [including European territory]	4,931,226 [whole country]	Tbilisi	Georgian
Oman	309,500	3,286,936	Muscat	Arabic
Armenia	29,743	3,056,382	Yerevan	Armenian
Mongolia	1,564,116	2,992,908	Ulan Bator	Mongolian
Kuwait	17,818	2,788,534	Kuwait City	Arabic
Qatar	11,586	2,194,817	Doha	Arabic
Bahrain	760	1,346,613	Manama	Arabic
East Timor	14,874	1,231,116	Dili	Portuguese, Tetum
Bhutan	38,394	741,919	Thimphu	Dzongkha
Brunei	5,765	429,646	Bandar Seri Begawan	Malay
Maldives	298	393,253	Malé	Dhivehi

Glossary

civilisations
communities that are well-organised with advanced social developments, often forming the basis for later nations

colonial
relating to the colonies – countries or areas controlled by another country and occupied by settlers from that country

empire
a group of countries governed under a single authority, such as under one ruler or country

Equator
an imaginary line drawn around the Earth separating the Northern and Southern hemispheres

exporter
a person, business or country that sells goods to another country

ger
a circular tent built with a framework of poles covered in felt or animal skins, used by nomadic people in Mongolia

humid subtropical
a climate zone characterised by hot, humid summers and mild to cool winters

meditation
spending time in quiet thought for religious purposes, concentration or relaxation

Mediterranean
a climate zone with long, hot and dry summers and cool, wet winters

nomadic
roaming about from place to place; describing the lifestyle of people and tribes who live in no fixed place, but move their homes around different parts of their country

pilgrimage
a journey to a special place, such as a site of religious importance

plantations
areas where a specific crop is grown on a large scale

polar
a climate zone found surrounding the North and South Poles, which are extremely cold and dry

rituals
acts that are always performed in the same sequence often as a ceremony that has spiritual or religious significance

shrine
a place or monument that is connected to religion and where people visit to perform an act of worship

Soviet Union
the Union of Soviet Socialist Republics (USSR), a former country that included Russia and countries from central Asia and eastern Europe

steppe
a large area of unforested grassland

subarctic
a climate zone that is found in areas of the Arctic Circle, experiencing long, cold winters and short, cool to mild summers

terraces
a series of flat areas that are formed or built like steep steps on a slope or hillside

textiles
material woven or knitted together, such as cloth

transcontinental
something that crosses over into more than one continent, such as the borders of a country or a railway line

tropical
a climate zone with hot and humid weather and high temperatures throughout the year

Index